# NUMBER CIRCUITS Level B

www.MINDWAREonline.com

# A MindWare® Original!

Our entire selection of Brainy Toys for Kids of All Ages® is available at www.MINDWAREonline.com, or by calling us at 800-999-0398 to request a catalog.

## Coloring Books

Each of our coloring books offer one of a kind patterns, textures and styles you make your own by choosing how to bring them to life.

**Animal Habitats Series**

**Creature Camouflage Series**

**Designs Series**

**Lights Series**

**Modern Patterns Series**

**Mosaics Series**

**Quilts Series**

**Scapes Series**

**Transformations Series**

## Puzzle Books

Our puzzle books build skills in many areas—from logic to math, spatial reasoning to verbal skills.

**Addition Adventures**

**Analogy Challenges**

**Clip Clue Puzzles**

**Code Breakers**

**Decimal Destinations**

**Deducibles**

**Directive Detective**

**Division Designs**

**Fast Fact Trivia**

**Fraction Finders**

**Grid Perplexors**

**Logic Links**

**Math Path Puzzles**

**Math Perplexors**

**More Multiplication Mosaics**

**Multiplication Mosaics**

**Noodlers**

**Number Circuits**

**Number Junctions**

**Perplexors**

**Sequencers**

**Subtraction Secrets**

**Tactic Twisters**

**Tan-Tastic Tangrams**

**Venn Perplexors**

**Word Winks**

**Word Wise**

## Games and Activities

Building blocks to strategic games, mystery puzzles to imaginative play — enhance abstract thinking and reasoning skills with our ingenious games and activities.

**Bella's Mystery Decks**

**Blik-Blok**

**Block Buddies**

**Chaos**

**Cross-Eyed**

**Flip 4**

**Gambit**

**Hue Knew?**

**Logic Links Game**

**Make Your Own Mask Kit**

**Noodlers Game**

**Pattern Play**

**Qwirkle**

**Tally Rally**

## Squzzles

Configure nine 3 x 3 pieces into a square where all images match up on every single side. Three challenging puzzles per box.

**3-D Scramblers**

**Animal Babies**

**Botanicals**

**Creature Kingdom**

**Creepy Crawlers**

**Dinosaurs!**

**Illusions**

**Insect Infested**

**Nocturnal Animals**

**Optical Illusions**

**Play Ball!**

**Wings & Wheels**

**World Money**

© 2008 MindWare Holdings, Inc.

Written by John L. Lehet
Editing by Eric Benjamin
Design by Muddpuppy

All rights reserved. Printed in the U.S.A.

Limited reproduction permission. The publisher grants permission to reproduce up to 100 copies of any part of this book for noncommercial classroom or individual use. Any further duplication is prohibited.

EAN 978-1-933054-6-12
SKU 36025

for other MindWare products visit our website
www.MINDWAREonline.com

# Number Circuits

Number Circuits Puzzles come in all sizes and shapes, including squares, circles, triangles, lines and many other geometric shapes. Number Circuits require the puzzler to arrange the provided numbers in a specific order and shape. They require and develop mental arithmetic skills, including addition and subtraction, as well as number familiarity.

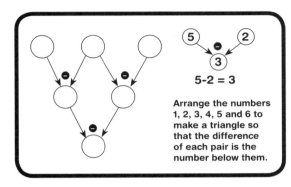

5-2 = 3

Arrange the numbers 1, 2, 3, 4, 5 and 6 to make a triangle so that the difference of each pair is the number below them.

In the puzzle to the left, the numbers 1 through 6 must be placed in each of the six circles. Each number must be placed into a circle so it is the difference of the two numbers pointing to it.

It's interesting that, in this puzzle, 6 can't be the bottom number and it can't be in the middle row, since it can never be the difference between any two of the other five numbers. So, 6 must be in the top row. This is just an example of how to start a puzzle.

Throughout the puzzles, there are often arithmetic signs (e.g. +, -) next to a circle. These indicate how the two numbers adjacent or pointing to the circle should be combined.

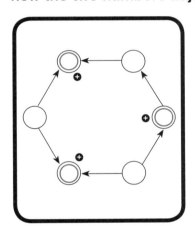

In the hexagon to the left, the "+" next to the gray circles indicate that the number to be placed into each is the "sum" of the two adjacent circles.

In the diamond to the right, the number in the top circle is the sum (+) of the two circles pointing to it. The number in the bottom circle is the difference (-) of the two circles pointing to it. The number in the center is the difference (-) of the numbers in the top and bottom circles.

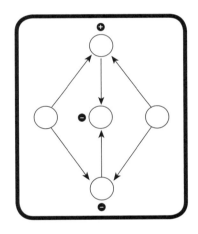

In many puzzles, the "difference" of two numbers is often asked for. It is important to note that the difference between two numbers is always positive. Although 2-5 is not positive, the difference between 2 and 5 is the same as the difference between 5 and 2, which is 3. Therefore, unless specifically stated, when the difference of two numbers is called for, the larger number does not have to be on the left side. In the example on the right, both are valid.

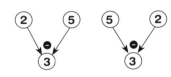

Number Circuits Puzzles are unique, fun, instructive and challenging. When tackling and solving them, children will get a deserved sense of arithmetic accomplishment and success.

# 1 Circuit Triangle

Arrange the numbers 1 through 10 to make a triangle so that the combination of each pair is the number below them.

**Example**
5 − 2 = 3

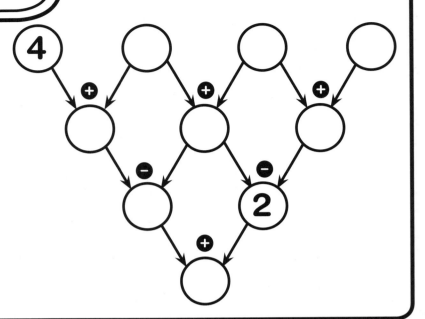

# 2 Circuit Triangle

Arrange the numbers 1 through 10 to make a triangle so that the combination of each pair is the number below them.

**Example**
5 − 2 = 3

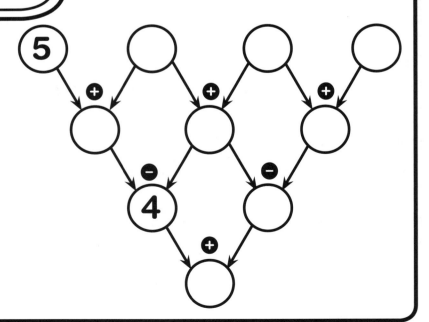

# 3 Circuit Triangle

Arrange the numbers 1 through 10 to make a triangle so that the combination of each pair is the number below them.

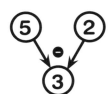

**Example**
5 – 2 = 3

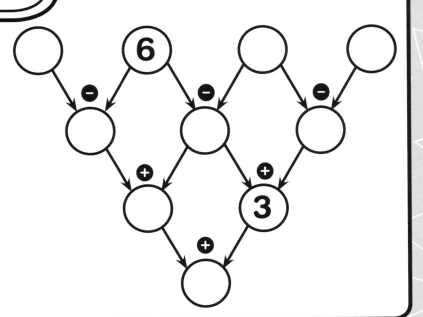

# 4 Circuit Triangle

Arrange the numbers 1 through 10 to make a triangle so that the combination of each pair is the number below them.

**Example**
5 – 2 = 3

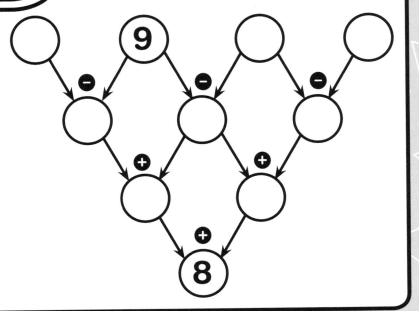

# Circuit Triangle

Arrange the numbers 1 through 10 to make a triangle so that the combination of each pair is the number below them.

**Example**
5 – 2 = 3

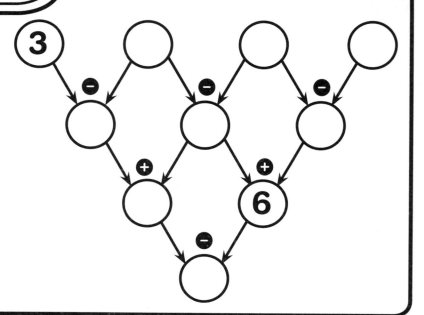

# Circuit Triangle

Arrange the numbers 1 through 10 to make a triangle so that the combination of each pair is the number below them.

**Example**
5 – 2 = 3

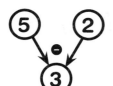

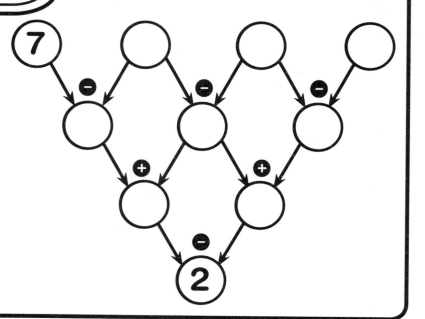

## 7  Circuit Triangle

Arrange the numbers 1 through 10 to make a triangle so that the combination of each pair is the number below them.

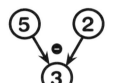

**Example**
5 − 2 = 3

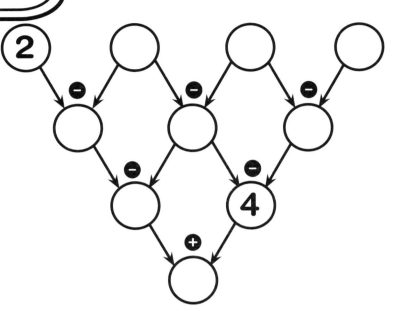

## 8  Circuit Triangle

Arrange the numbers 1 through 10 to make a triangle so that the combination of each pair is the number below them.

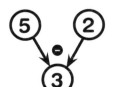

**Example**
5 − 2 = 3

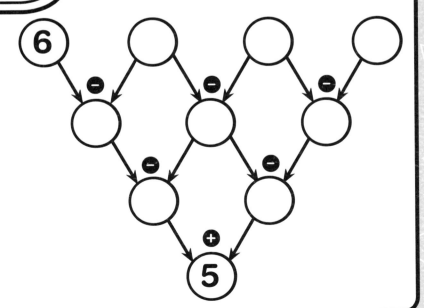

## 9 Circuit Triangle

Arrange the numbers 1 through 10 to make a triangle so that the combination of each pair is the number below them.

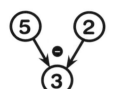

**Example**
5 − 2 = 3

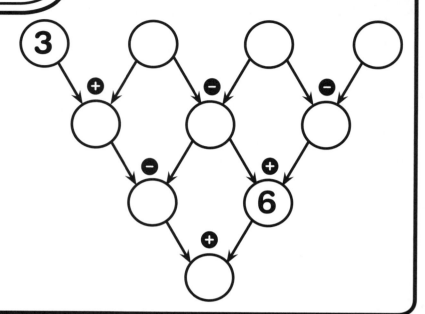

## 10 Circuit Triangle

Arrange the numbers 1 through 10 to make a triangle so that the combination of each pair is the number below them.

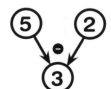

**Example**
5 − 2 = 3

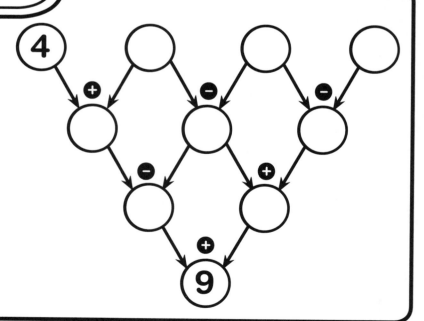

**Circuit Triangle**

Arrange the numbers 1, 2, 3, 4, 5, 6, 7, 8 and 9 to make a triangle so that the sum of the four numbers along each side is 17.

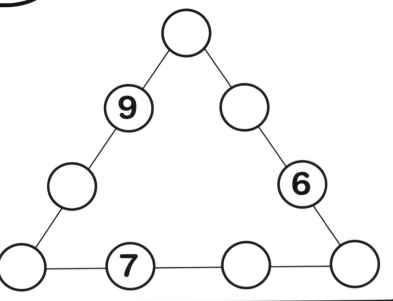

**12** **Circuit Triangle**

Arrange the numbers 1, 2, 3, 4, 5, 6, 7, 8 and 9 to make a triangle so that the sum of the four numbers along each side is 17.

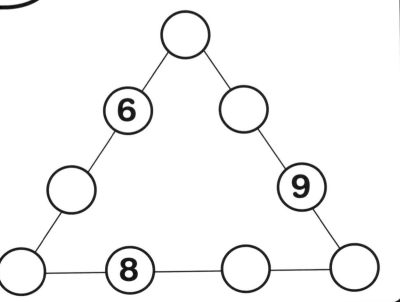

## 13 Circuit Triangle

Arrange the numbers 1, 2, 3, 4, 5, 6, and 7 to make three triangles so that the sum of the three numbers on the smallest triangle is 9 and equals the difference of the sum of the five numbers on the medium triangle and the sum of the seven numbers on the large triangle and the sums of the four numbers on each side are equal.

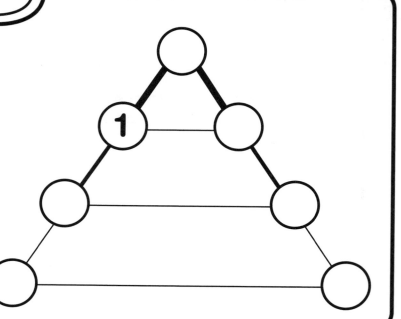

## 14 Circuit Triangle

Arrange the numbers 1, 2, 3, 4, 5, 6, and 7 to make three triangles so that the sum of the three numbers on the smallest triangle is 8 and equals the difference of the sum of the five numbers on the medium triangle and the sum of the seven numbers on the large triangle and the sums of the four numbers on each side are equal.

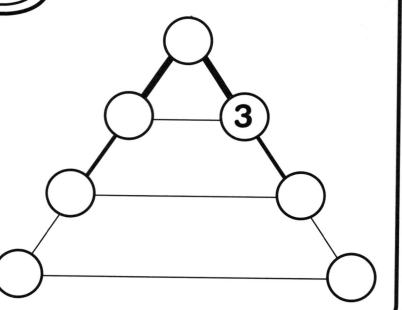

## 15 Circuit Triangle

Arrange the numbers 1, 2, 3, 4, 5, 6, and 7 to make three triangles so that the sum of the three numbers on the smallest triangle is 12 and equals the difference of the sum of the five numbers on the medium triangle and the sum of the seven numbers on the large triangle and the sums of the four numbers on each side are equal.

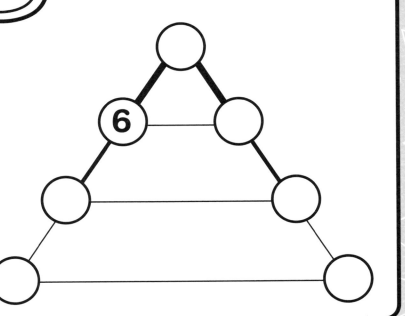

## 16 Circuit Triangle

Arrange the numbers 1, 2, 3, 4, 5, 6, and 7 to make three triangles so that the sum of the three numbers on the smallest triangle is 11 and equals the difference of the sum of the five numbers on the medium triangle and the sum of the seven numbers on the large triangle and the sums of the four numbers on each side are equal.

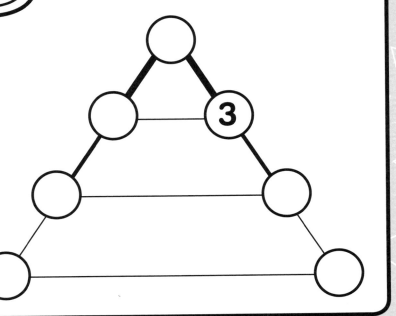

Arrange the numbers 1, 2, 3, 4, 5, 6, 7 and 8 so that the sum of the four numbers on each of the three large triangles is the same.

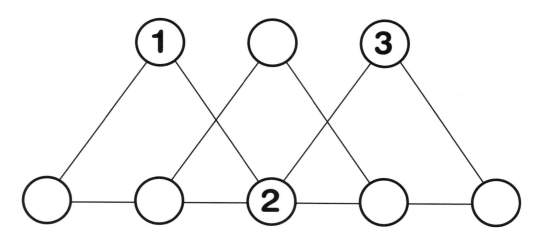

Arrange the numbers 1, 2, 3, 4, 5, 6, 7 and 8 so that the sum of the four numbers on each of the three large triangles is 21.

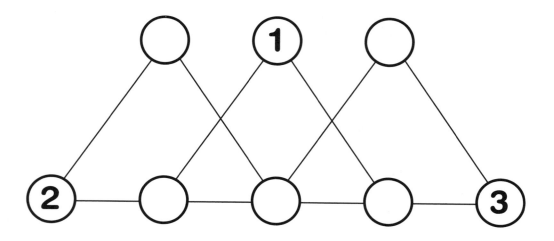

## 19  Circuit Triangle

Arrange the numbers 1, 2, 3, 4, 5, 6, 7 and 8 so that the sum of the four numbers on each of the three large triangles is 16.

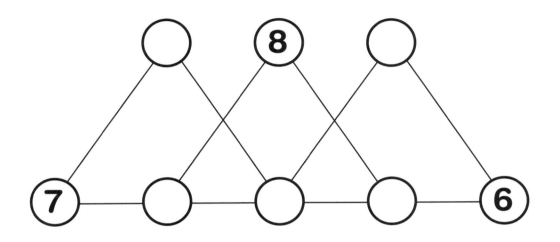

## 20  Circuit Triangle

Arrange the numbers 1, 2, 3, 4, 5, 6, 7 and 8 so that the sum of the four numbers on each of the three large triangles is 15.

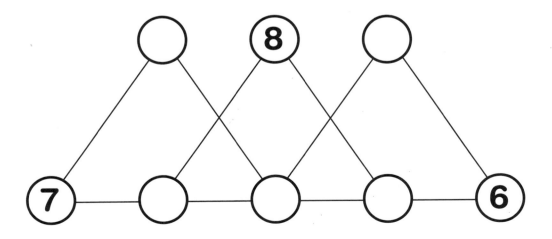

# 1 Circuit Hexagon

Arrange the numbers 1, 2, 3, 4, 6 and 8 to make a hexagon so that the gray circles are the indicated combinations of the two adjacent white circles.

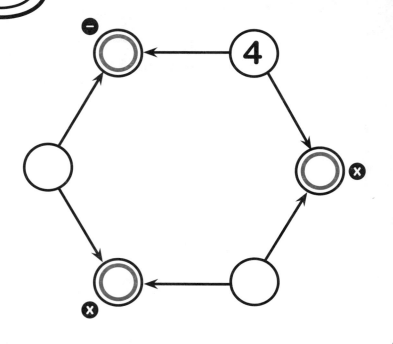

# 2 Circuit Hexagon

Arrange the numbers 2, 4, 6, 8, 12 and 16 to make a hexagon so that the gray circles are the indicated combinations of the two adjacent white circles.

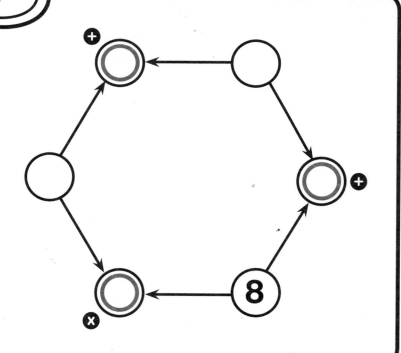

## 3 Circuit Hexagon

Arrange the numbers 1, 2, 3, 4, 5 and 8 to make a hexagon so that the gray circles are the indicated combinations of the two adjacent white circles.

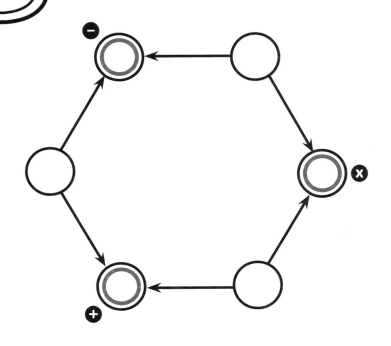

## 4 Circuit Hexagon

Arrange the numbers 1, 2, 3, 4, 6 and 12 to make a hexagon so that the gray circles are the indicated combinations of the two adjacent white circles.

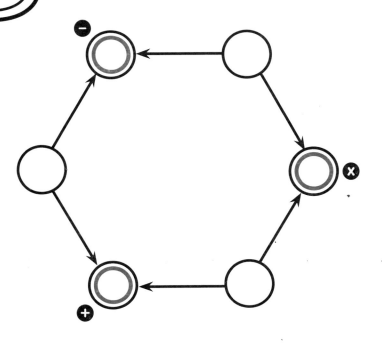

## 5 Circuit Hexagon

Arrange the numbers 1, 2, 3, 4, 5 and 12 to make a hexagon so that the gray circles are the indicated combinations of the two adjacent white circles.

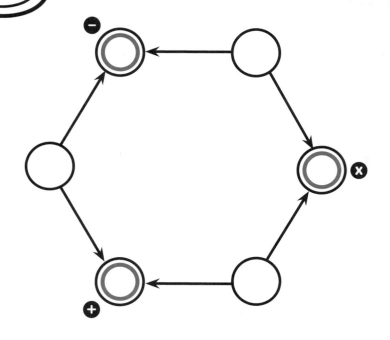

## 6 Circuit Hexagon

Arrange the numbers 2, 4, 6, 8, 10 and 12 to make a hexagon so that the gray circles are the indicated combinations of the two adjacent white circles.

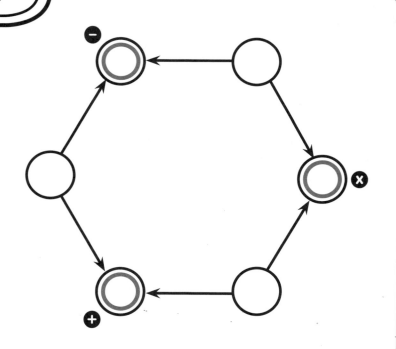

# 7 Circuit Hexagon

Arrange the numbers 1, 2, 3, 5, 8 and 13 to make a hexagon so that the sum of the top three numbers equals the sum of the bottom three numbers **and** the top number is the sum of the two adjacent numbers **and** the sum of the left two numbers is 6.

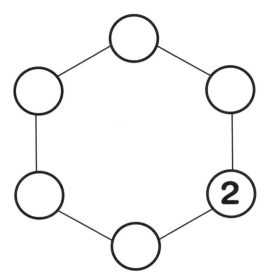

# 8 Circuit Hexagon

Arrange the numbers 2, 3, 5, 7, 11 and 13 to make a hexagon so that the sum of the top three numbers is 18 **and** the sum of the left two numbers is 20 **and** the sum of the right two numbers is 8.

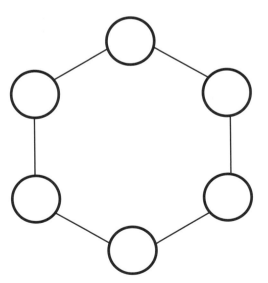

## 1 Circuit Pentagon

Arrange the numbers 1, 2, 3, 4 and 5 to make a pentagon so that the sum of the two right numbers equals the sum of the two left numbers and the top number is the difference of the bottom two numbers.

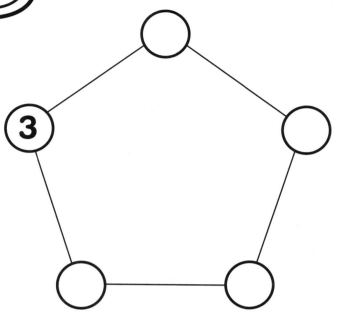

## 2 Circuit Pentagon

Arrange the numbers 1, 2, 3, 4 and 5 to make a pentagon so that the sum of the two right numbers equals the sum of the two left numbers and the top number is the difference of the bottom two numbers.

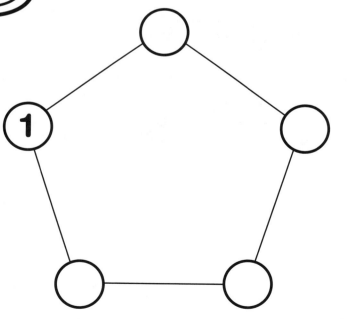

## 3 Circuit Pentagon

Arrange the numbers 1, 2, 3, 4 and 5 to make a pentagon so that the sum of the two right numbers equals the sum of the two left numbers and the top number is the sum of the bottom two numbers.

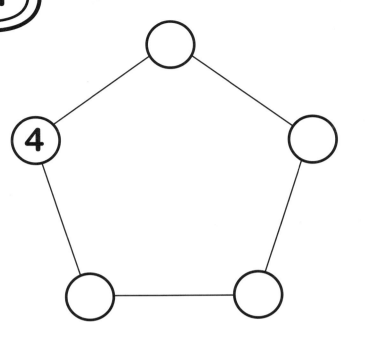

## 4 Circuit Pentagon

Arrange the numbers 1, 2, 3, 4 and 5 to make a pentagon so that the difference of the two right numbers equals the difference of the two left numbers and the top number is the sum of the bottom two numbers.

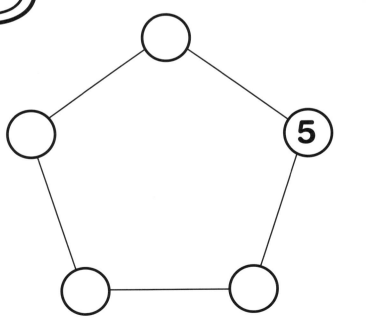

## 5 Circuit Pentagon

Arrange the numbers 1, 2, 3, 4 and 5 to make a pentagon so that the difference of the two right numbers equals the difference of the two left numbers and the top number is the difference of the bottom two numbers.

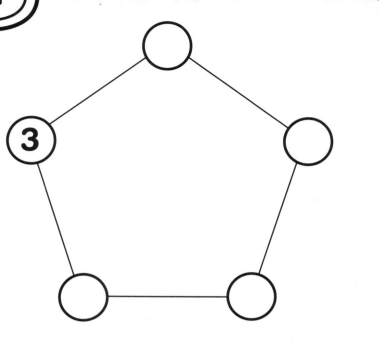

## 6 Circuit Pentagon

Arrange the numbers 1, 2, 3, 4 and 5 to make a pentagon so that the difference of the two right numbers equals the difference of the two left numbers and the top number is the difference of the bottom two numbers.

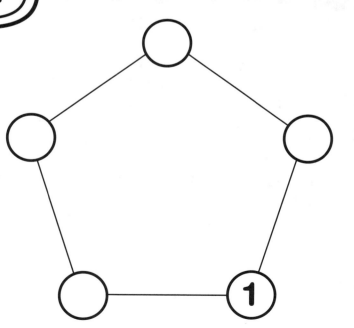

## Circuit Pentagon

Arrange the numbers 1, 2, 3, 4 and 5 to make a pentagon so that the difference of the two right numbers equals the difference of the two left numbers and the top number is half the difference of the bottom two numbers.

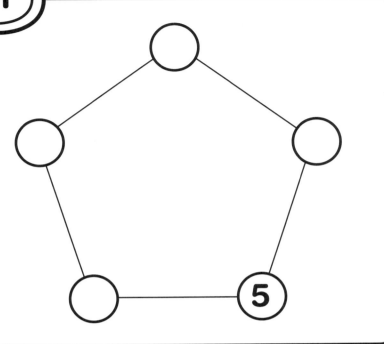

**8**

## Circuit Pentagon

Arrange the numbers 1, 2, 3, 4 and 5 to make a pentagon so that the difference of the two right numbers equals the difference of the two left numbers and the top number is half the difference of the bottom two numbers.

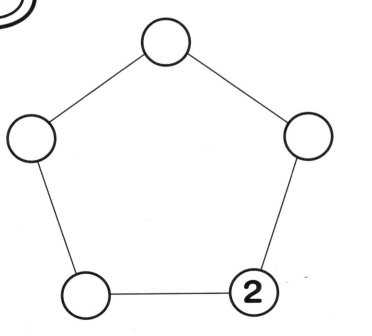

# 1 Circuit Circles

Arrange the numbers 1, 2, 3, 4, 5 and 6 so that the combination of the four numbers on each of the two large circles is 7.

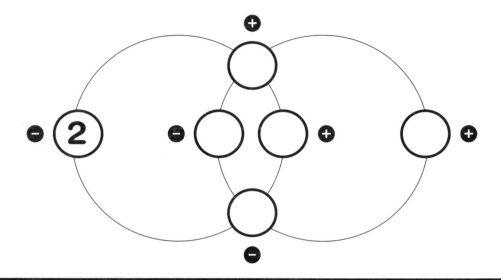

# 2 Circuit Circles

Arrange the numbers 1, 2, 3, 4, 5 and 6 so that the combination of the four numbers on each of the two large circles is 1.

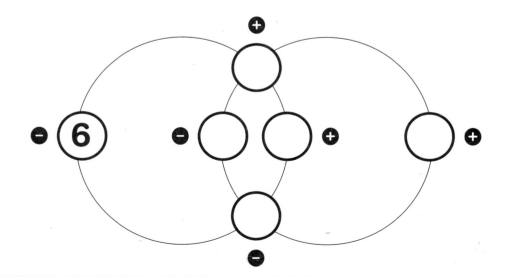

## 3 Circuit Circles

Arrange the numbers 1, 2, 3, 4, 5 and 6 so that the combination of the four numbers on each of the two large circles is 1.

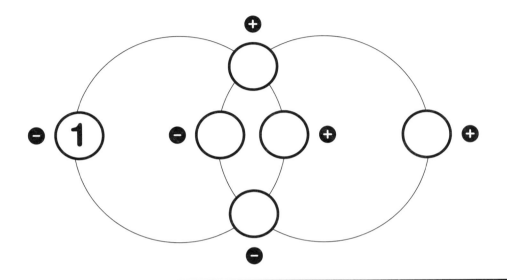

## 4 Circuit Circles

Arrange the numbers 1, 2, 3, 4, 5 and 6 so that the combination of the four numbers on each of the two large circles is 2.

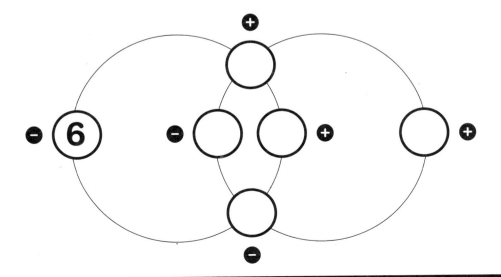

## 5 Circuit Circles

Arrange the numbers
1 through 7 in the small
circles so that the indicated
combination of the four
numbers in each of the
three large circles is 2.

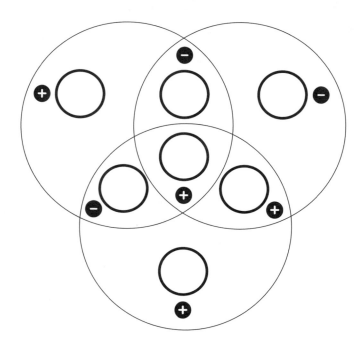

## 6 Circuit Circles

Arrange the numbers
1 through 7 in the small
circles so that the indicated
combination of the four
numbers in each of the
three large circles is 3.

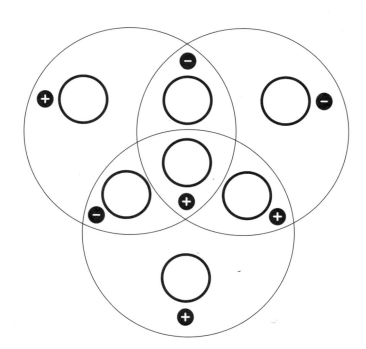

## 7 Circuit Circles

Arrange the numbers 1 through 7 in the small circles so that the indicated combination of the four numbers in each of the three large circles is 4.

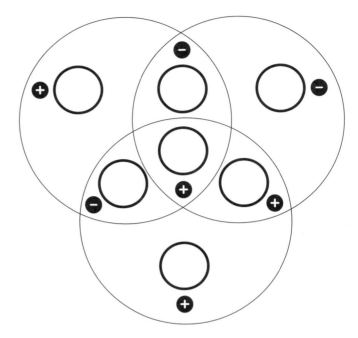

## 8 Circuit Circles

Arrange the numbers 1 through 7 in the small circles so that the indicated combination of the four numbers in each of the three large circles is 5.

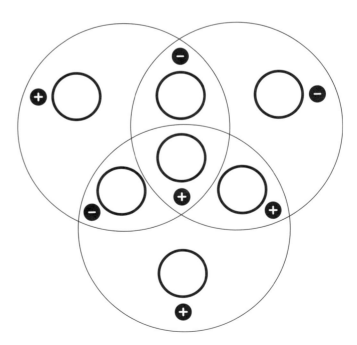

## 9  Circuit Circles

Arrange the numbers 1 through 9 in the small circles so that the indicated combination of the five numbers on each of the three large circles is 1.

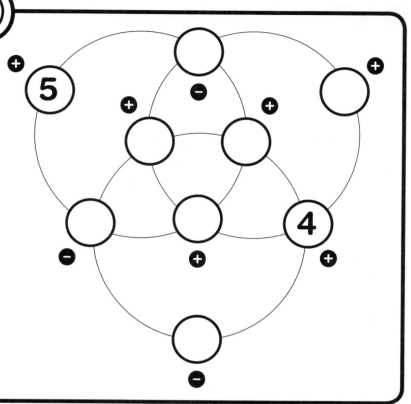

## 10  Circuit Circles

Arrange the numbers 1 through 9 in the small circles so that the indicated combination of the five numbers on each of the three large circles is 2.

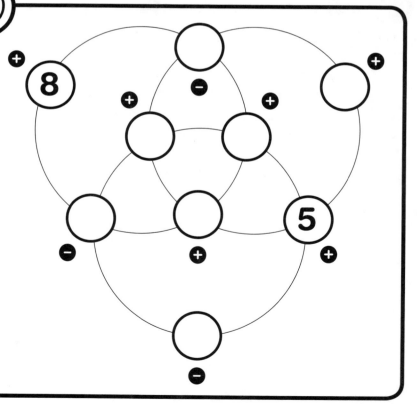

## 11 Circuit Circles

Arrange the numbers 1 through 9 in the small circles so that the indicated combination of the five numbers on each of the three large circles is 16.

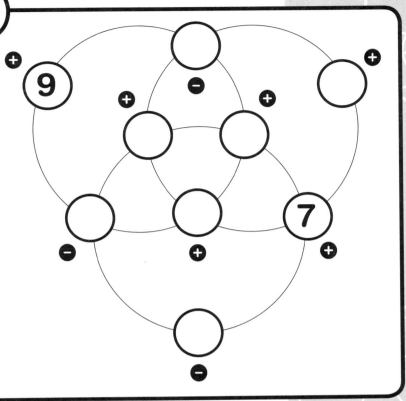

## 12 Circuit Circles

Arrange the numbers 1 through 9 in the small circles so that the indicated combination of the five numbers on each of the three large circles is 17.

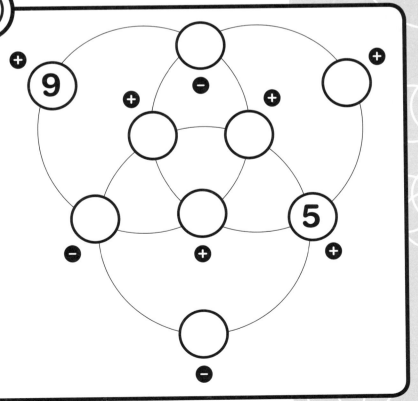

## 13 Circuit Circles

Arrange the numbers 1, 2, 3, 4, 5, 6, 7, 8 and 9 so that the sum of the numbers in each of the four large circles is 19 **and** the sum of the four numbers in each row are equal.

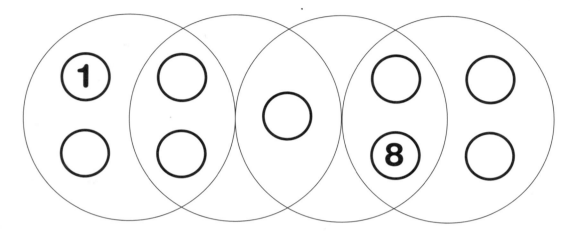

## 14 Circuit Circles

Arrange the numbers 1, 2, 3, 4, 5, 6, 7, 8 and 9 so that the sum of the numbers in each of the four large circles is 20 **and** the sum of the four numbers in each row are equal.

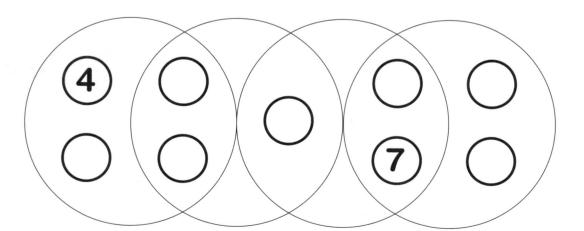

# Circuit Circles

Arrange the numbers 1, 2, 3, 4, 5, 6, 7, 8 and 9 so that the sum of the numbers in each of the four large circles is 20 **and** the sum of the four numbers in each row are equal.

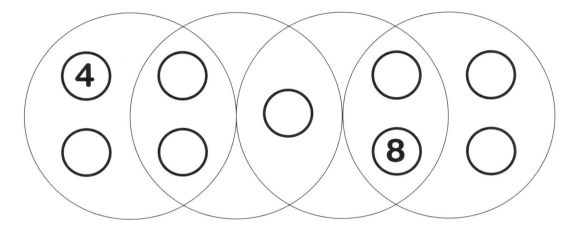

---

# 16 Circuit Circles

Arrange the numbers 1, 2, 3, 4, 5, 6, 7, 8 and 9 so that the sum of the numbers in each of the four large circles is 18 **and** the sum of the four numbers in each row are equal.

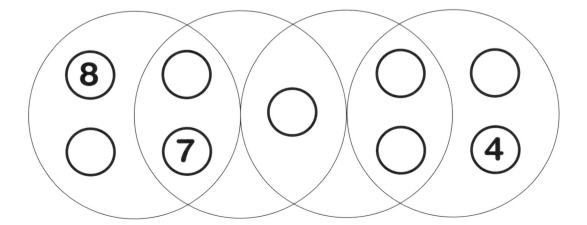

## 17  Circuit Circles

Arrange the numbers 1, 2, 3, 4, 5, 6, 7 and 8 so that the sum of the four numbers in each of the four large circles is 16.

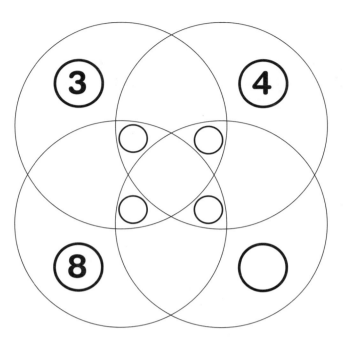

## 18  Circuit Circles

Arrange the numbers 1, 2, 3, 4, 5, 6, 7 and 8 so that the sum of the four numbers in each of the four large circles is 17.

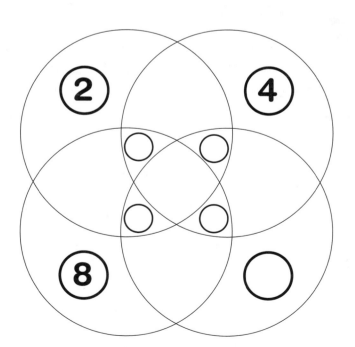

## 19 Circuit Circles

Arrange the numbers 1, 2, 3, 4, 5, 6, 7 and 8 so that the sum of the four numbers in each of the four large circles is 19.

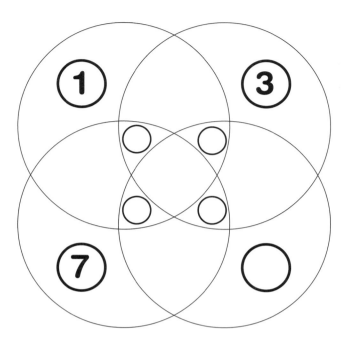

## 20 Circuit Circles

Arrange the numbers 1, 2, 3, 4, 5, 6, 7 and 8 so that the sum of the four numbers in each of the four large circles is 20.

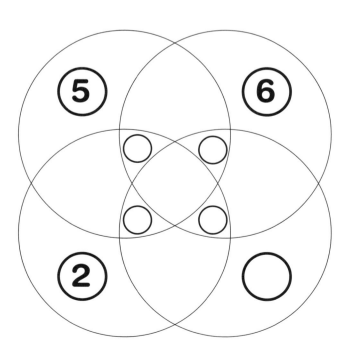

## 1 Circuit Squares

Arrange the numbers 1, 2, 3, 4, 5, 6, and 7 so the sum of the four numbers on the corners of each square is 16 **and** the sums of the numbers in the horizontal line of three and the vertical line of three are both 12.

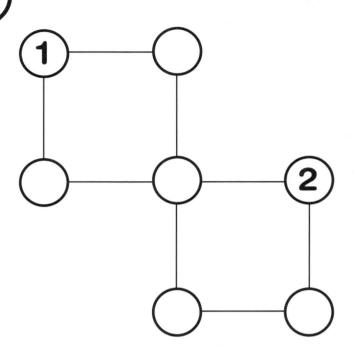

## 2 Circuit Squares

Arrange the numbers 1, 2, 3, 4, 5, 6, and 7 so the sum of the four numbers on the corners of each square is 15 **and** the sums of the numbers in the horizontal line of three and the vertical line of three are both 13.

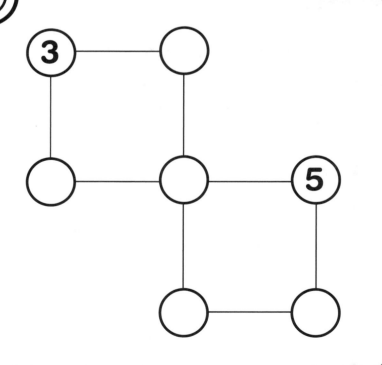

## 3 Circuit Squares

Arrange the numbers 1, 2, 3, 4, 5, 6, and 7 so the sum of the four numbers on the corners of each square is 17 **and** the sums of the numbers in the horizontal line of three and the vertical line of three are both 11.

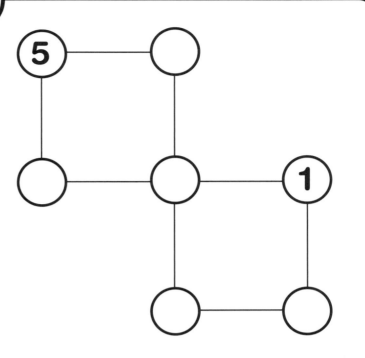

## 4 Circuit Squares

Arrange the numbers 1, 2, 3, 4, 5, 6, and 7 so the sum of the four numbers on the corners of each square is 16 **and** the sums of the numbers in the horizontal line of three and the vertical line of three are both 12.

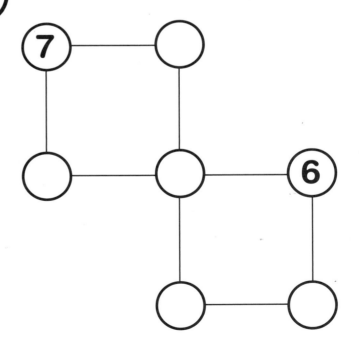

## 5 Circuit Squares

Arrange the numbers 1, 2, 3, 4, 5, 6, and 7 so the sum of the four numbers on the corners of the bottom square is twice the sum of the four numbers on the top square **and** the sums of the numbers in the horizontal line of three and the vertical line of three are both 14.

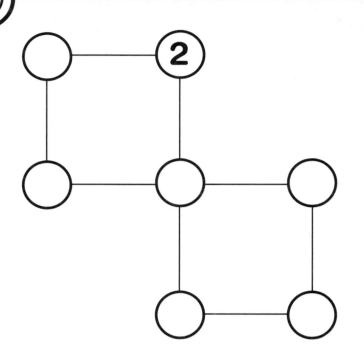

## 6 Circuit Squares

Arrange the numbers 1, 2, 3, 4, 5, 6, and 7 so the sum of the four numbers on the corners of the bottom square is twice the sum of the four numbers on the top square **and** the sums of the numbers in the horizontal line of three and the vertical line of three are both 13.

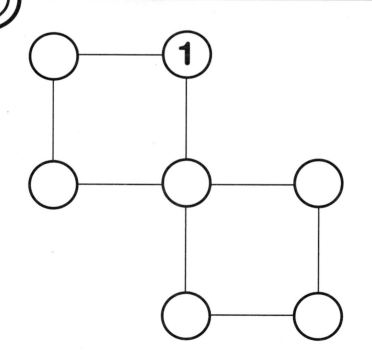

## 7 Circuit Squares

Arrange the numbers 1, 2, 3, 4, 5, 6, and 7 so the sum of the four numbers on the corners of the bottom square is twice the sum of the four numbers on the top square **and** the sums of the numbers in the horizontal line of three and the vertical line of three are both 11.

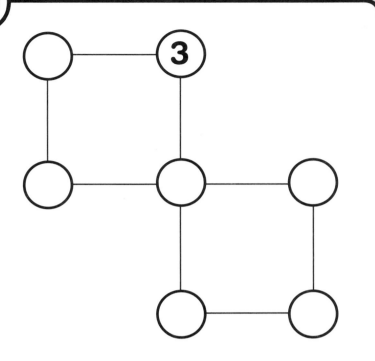

## 8 Circuit Squares

Arrange the numbers 1, 2, 3, 4, 5, 6, and 7 so the sum of the four numbers on the corners of the bottom square is twice the sum of the four numbers on the top square **and** the sums of the numbers in the horizontal line of three and the vertical line of three are both 10.

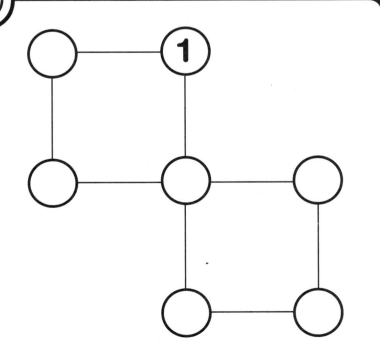

## 1 Circuit Connection

Arrange the numbers 2, 3, 4, 6, 8, 9 and 12 so that the numbers in each gray circle are factors of the number in each adjacent white circle **and** the number in the center gray circle is the difference of the two numbers in the adjacent white circles.

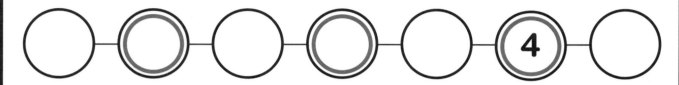

## 2 Circuit Connection

Arrange the numbers 2, 4, 5, 8, 10, 15 and 20 so that the numbers in each gray circle are factors of the number in each adjacent white circle **and** the number in the center gray circle is the difference of the two numbers in the adjacent white circles.

## 3 Circuit Connection

Arrange the prime numbers 3, 5, 7, 11, 13 and 17 so that adjacent numbers have no digits in common **and** the sum of the two numbers in the gray circles is 16.

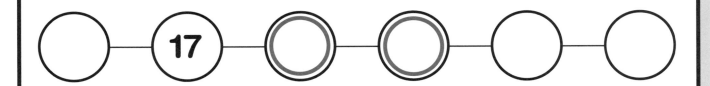

## 4 Circuit Connection

Arrange the prime numbers 3, 5, 7, 11, 13 and 17 so that adjacent numbers have no digits in common **and** the sum of the two numbers in the gray circles is 18.

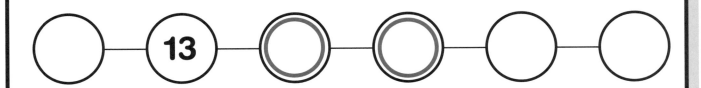

## 5 Circuit Connection

Arrange the numbers 2, 3, 4, 6, 8 and 12 so that the number in each gray circle is the difference or product as indicated of the numbers in its two adjacent circles.

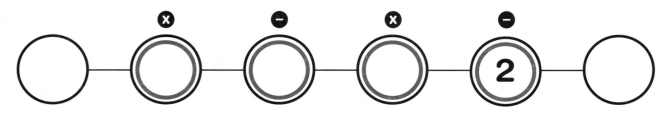

## 6 Circuit Connection

Arrange the numbers 2, 3, 4, 8, 9 and 12 so that the number in each gray circle is the difference or product as indicated of the numbers in its two adjacent circles.

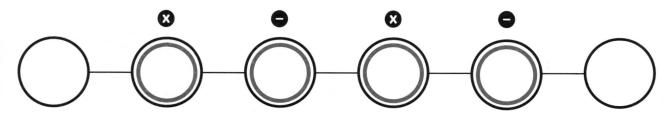

## 7 Circuit Connection

Arrange the numbers 2, 3, 4, 6, 8 and 12 so that the number in each gray circle is the difference or product as indicated of the numbers in its two adjacent circles.

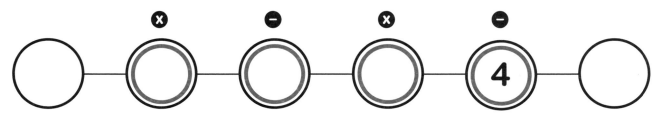

## 8 Circuit Connection

Arrange the numbers 2, 4, 5, 8, 10 and 12 so that the number in each gray circle is the difference or product as indicated of the numbers in its two adjacent circles.

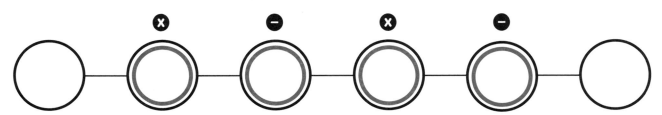

# 1 Circuit Octagon

Arrange the numbers 1, 2, 3, 4, 5, 6, 7 and 8 to make an octagon so that the sums of the four numbers in the top half, the bottom half, the left half, and the right half are all equal and the sum of the top two numbers is 10 and the sum of the bottom two numbers is 12.

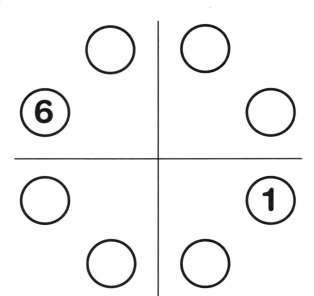

# 2 Circuit Octagon

Arrange the numbers 1, 2, 3, 4, 5, 6, 7 and 8 to make an octagon so that the sums of the four numbers in the top half, the bottom half, the left half, and the right half are all equal and opposite quadrants are equal and the sum of the top two numbers is 8 and the sum of the bottom two numbers is 5.

## 3 Circuit Octagon

Arrange the numbers 1, 2, 3, 4, 5, 6, 7 and 8 to make an octagon so that the sum of the bottom four numbers is 23 and the sum of the right four numbers is 22 and no consecutive numbers are in adjacent circles.

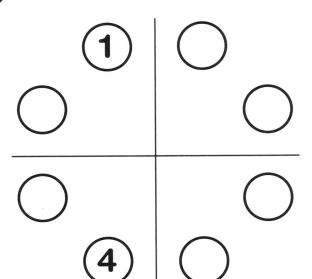

## 4 Circuit Octagon

Arrange the numbers 1, 2, 3, 4, 5, 6, 7 and 8 to make an octagon so that the sum of the bottom four numbers is 11 and the sum of the left four numbers is 21 and no consecutive numbers are in adjacent circles.

## 5 Circuit Octagon

Arrange the numbers 1, 2, 3, 4, 5, 6, 7 and 8 to make an octagon so that the sums of the four numbers in the top half, the bottom half, the left half, and the right half are all equal and the sum of the top two numbers is 10 and the sum of the bottom two numbers is 12.

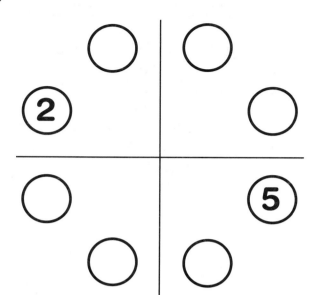

## 6 Circuit Octagon

Arrange the numbers 1, 2, 3, 4, 5, 6, 7 and 8 to make an octagon so that the sums of the four numbers in the top half, the bottom half, the left half, and the right half are all equal and the sum of the top two numbers is 8 and the sum of the bottom two numbers is 7.

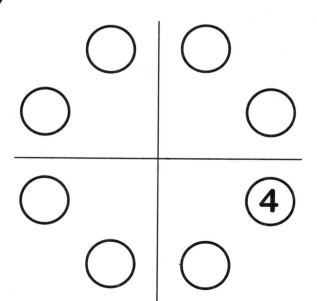

## 7 Circuit Octagon

Arrange the numbers 1, 2, 3, 4, 5, 6, 7 and 8 to make an octagon so that the sums of the four numbers in the top half, the bottom half, the left half, and the right half are all equal and the sum of the top two numbers is 8 and the sum of the bottom two numbers is 7.

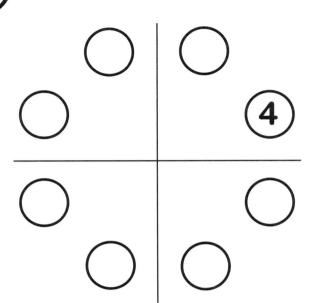

## 8 Circuit Octagon

Arrange the numbers 1, 2, 3, 4, 5, 6, 7 and 8 to make an octagon so that the sum of the bottom four numbers is 11 and the sum of the left four numbers is 21 and no consecutive numbers are in adjacent circles.

# 1  Circuit Septagon

Arrange the numbers
1, 2, 3, 4, 5, 6 and 8 to
make a septagon so each
gray circle is the indicated
combination of the two
adjacent white circles

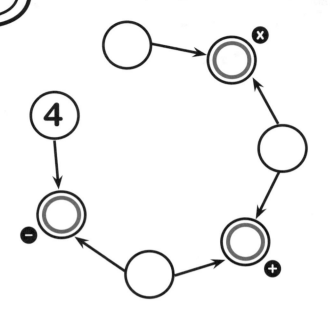

# 2  Circuit Septagon

Arrange the numbers
1, 2, 3, 4, 5, 6 and 8 to
make a septagon so each
gray circle is the indicated
combination of the two
adjacent white circles

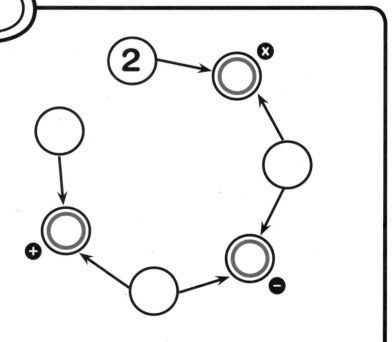

## 3 Circuit Septagon

Arrange the numbers
1, 2, 3, 4, 5, 6 and 8 to
make a septagon so each
gray circle is the indicated
combination of the two
adjacent white circles

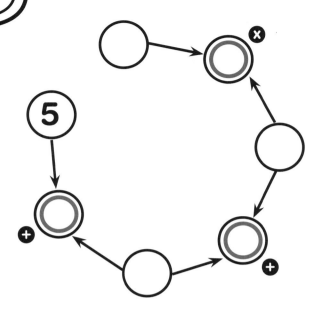

## 4 Circuit Septagon

Arrange the numbers
1, 2, 3, 4, 5, 6 and 8 to
make a septagon so each
gray circle is the indicated
combination of the two
adjacent white circles

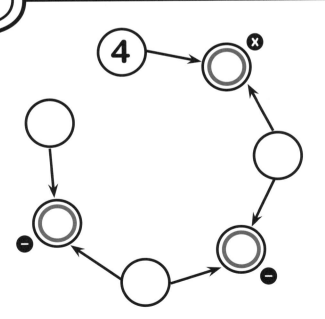

## 1 Circuit Star

Arrange the numbers 1, 2, 3, 4, 5, 6, 7, 8, 9 and 12 to make a star so each outer point is the difference of the two adjacent numbers.

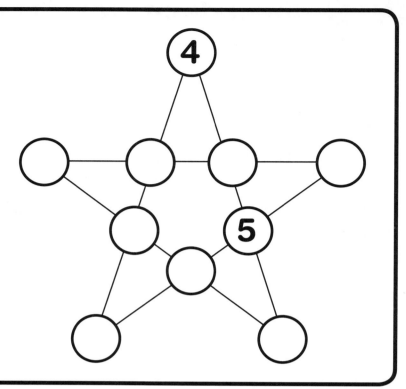

## 2 Circuit Star

Arrange the numbers 1, 2, 3, 4, 5, 6, 7, 8, 10 and 14 to make a star so each outer point is the difference of the two adjacent numbers.

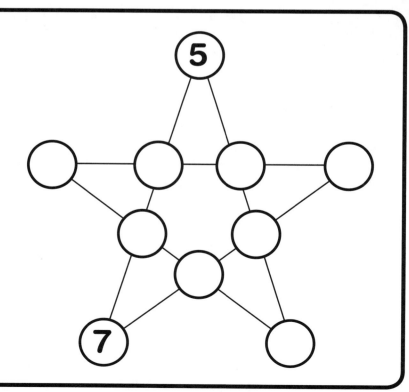

## 3 Circuit Star

Arrange the numbers 1, 2, 3, 4, 5, 6, 7, 8, 9 and 12 to make a star so each outer point is the difference of the two adjacent numbers.

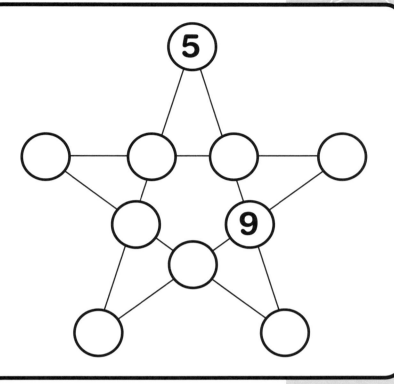

## 4 Circuit Star

Arrange the numbers 1, 2, 3, 4, 5, 6, 7, 8, 10 and 14 to make a star so each outer point is the difference of the two adjacent numbers.

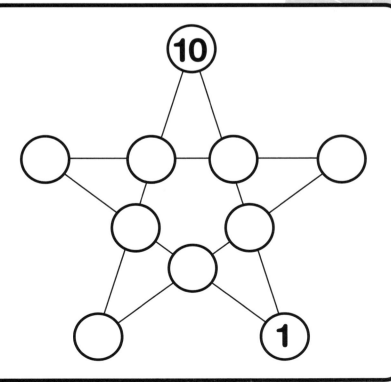

## 5 Circuit Star

Arrange the numbers 1, 2, 3, 4, 5, 6, 7, 8, 9 and 12 to make a star so each outer point is the indicated combination of the two adjacent numbers.

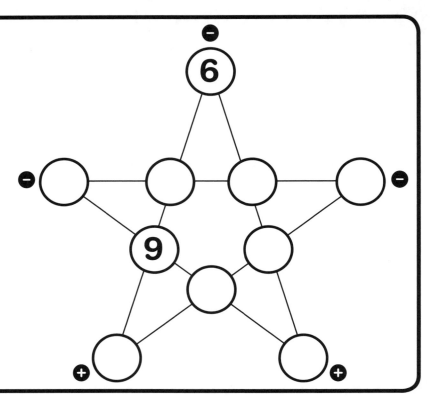

## 6 Circuit Star

Arrange the numbers 1, 2, 3, 4, 5, 6, 7, 8, 9 and 12 to make a star so each outer point is the indicated combination of the two adjacent numbers.

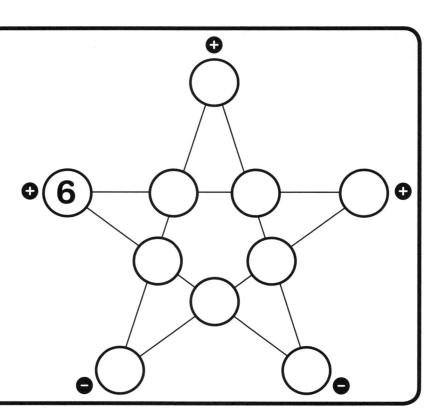

## 7 Circuit Star

Arrange the numbers 1, 2, 3, 4, 5, 6, 7, 8, 9 and 12 to make a star so each outer point is the indicated combination of the two adjacent numbers.

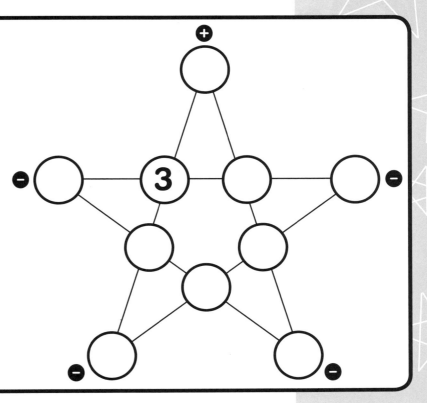

## 8 Circuit Star

Arrange the numbers 1, 2, 3, 4, 5, 6, 7, 8, 10 and 14 to make a star so each outer point is the indicated combination of the two adjacent numbers.

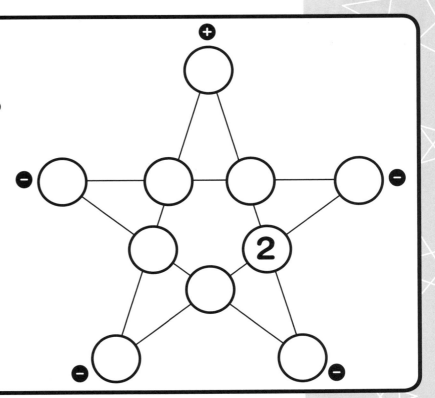

## 9 Circuit Star

Arrange the numbers 1, 2, 3, 4, 5, 6, 7, 8, 9 and 12 to make a star so each outer point is the indicated combination of the two adjacent numbers.

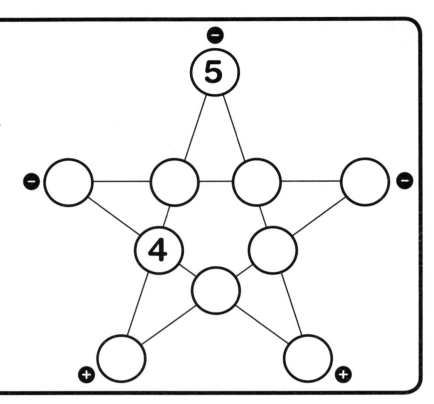

## 10 Circuit Star

Arrange the numbers 1, 2, 3, 4, 5, 6, 7, 8, 9 and 12 to make a star so each outer point is the indicated combination of the two adjacent numbers.

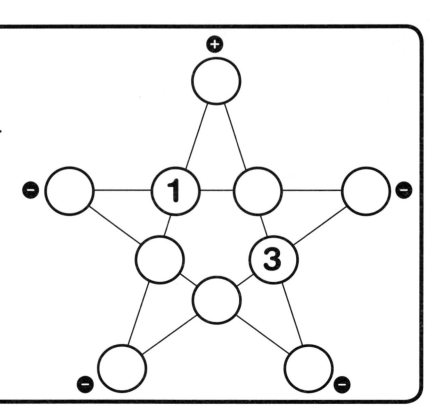

## 11 Circuit Star

Arrange the numbers 1, 2, 3, 4, 5, 6, 7, 8, 9 and 12 to make a star so each outer point is the indicated combination of the two adjacent numbers.

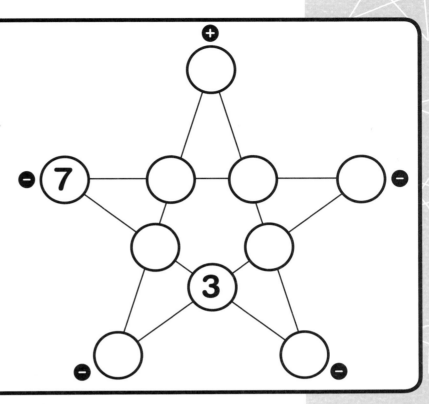

## 12 Circuit Star

Arrange the numbers 1, 2, 3, 4, 5, 6, 7, 8, 10 and 14 to make a star so each outer point is the indicated combination of the two adjacent numbers.

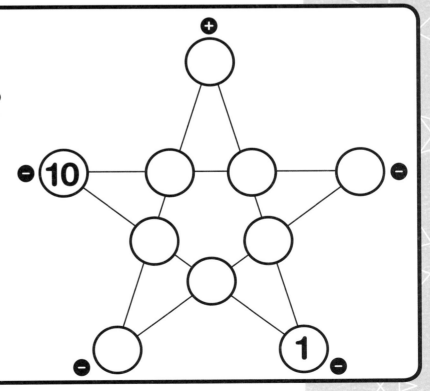

# Solutions

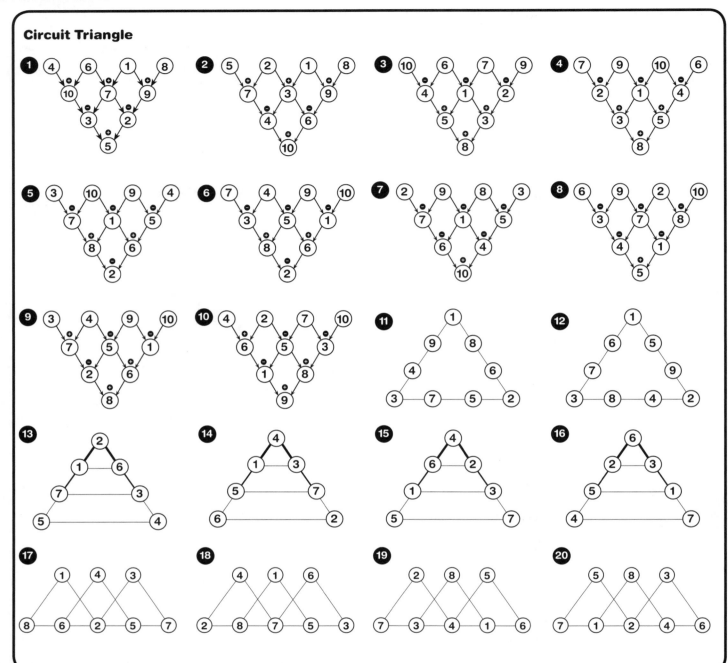

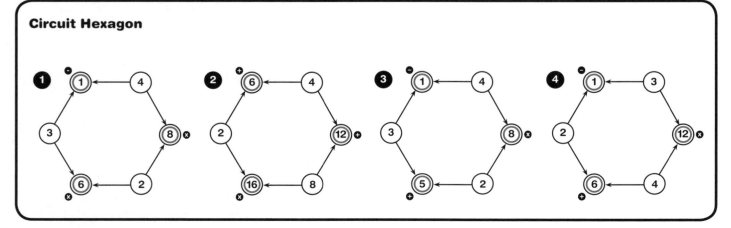

## Circuit Hexagon continued

 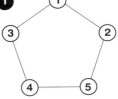
**5** 

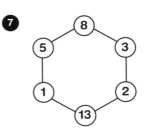
**6**

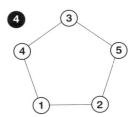
**7**

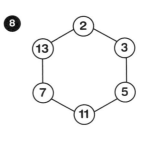
**8**

## Circuit Pentagon

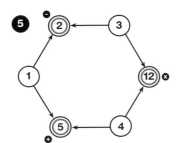
**1**

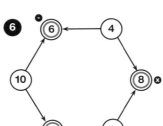
**2**

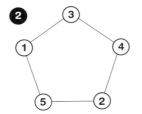
**3**

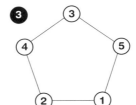
**4**

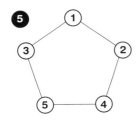
**5**

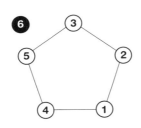
**6**

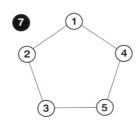
**7**

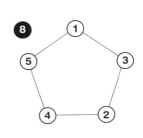
**8**

## Circuit Circles

**1**

**2**

**3**

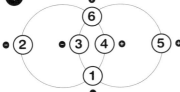
**4**

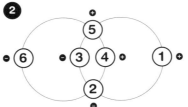  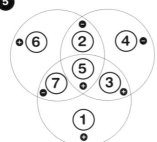
**5**

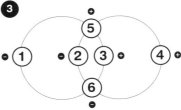 
**6**

**7**  + ⑦  ⊖ ②  ③ ⊖  ⊖ ⑥  ⑤ ⊕  ④ ⊕  ① ⊕

**8**  ⊕ ⑦  ⊖ ①  ③ ⊖  ⊖ ⑥  ⑤ ⊕  ④ ⊕  ② ⊕

**9**  ⊕ ⑤  ⑨  ① ⊕  ⊕ ②  ⊖ ⑧ ⊕  ⑥ ⊖  ③ ⊕  ④ ⊕  ⑦ ⊖

**10**  ⊕ ⑧  ⑨ ⊖  ③ ⊕  ⊕ ② ⊕  ⑥  ④ ⊖  ① ⊕  ⑤ ⊕  ⑦ ⊖

**11**  ⊕ ⑨  ④ ⊖  ② ⊕  ⊕ ⑤ ⊕  ⑧  ③ ⊖  ⑥ ⊕  ⑦ ⊕  ① ⊖

**12**  ⊕ ⑨  ④ ⊖  ③ ⊕  ⊕ ⑦ ⊕  ⑧  ② ⊖  ⑥ ⊕  ⑤ ⊕  ① ⊖

**13**  ① ⑨ ⑦ ④ ⑤  ⑥ ③ ⑧ ②

**14**  ④ ⑥ ⑤ ⑧ ②  ① ⑨ ⑦ ③

**15**  ④ ⑥ ⑤ ⑦ ③  ① ⑨ ⑧ ②

**16**  ⑧ ② ⑨ ③ ⑤  ① ⑦ ⑥ ④

**17**  ③ ④  ⑤ ⑥  ② ①  ⑧ ⑦

**18**  ② ④  ⑤ ⑦  ③ ①  ⑧ ⑥

**19**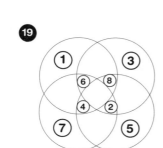

**20**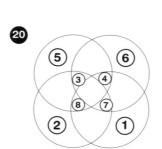

## Circuit Octagon

**1**

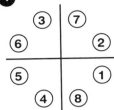

③ ⑦
⑥ ②
⑤ ①
④ ⑧

**2**

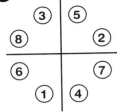

③ ⑤
⑧ ②
⑥ ⑦
① ④

**3**

① ⑦
③ ②
⑥ ⑤
④ ⑧

**4**

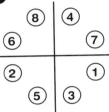

⑧ ④
⑥ ⑦
② ①
⑤ ③

**5**

⑦ ③
② ⑥
① ⑤
⑧ ④

**6**

③ ⑤
② ⑧
⑦ ④
⑥ ①

**7**

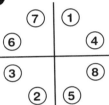

⑦ ①
⑥ ④
③ ⑧
② ⑤

**8**

⑧ ④
⑥ ⑦
② ③
⑤ ①

## Circuit Squares

**1**
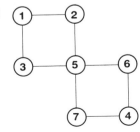

**2**

**3**
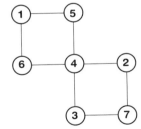

**4**
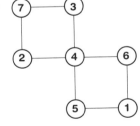

**5**

**6**
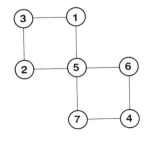

**7**
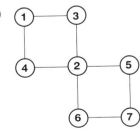

**8**
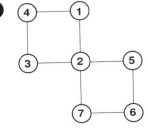

## Circuit Septagon

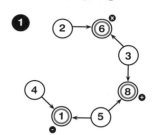 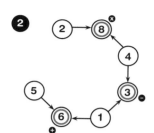 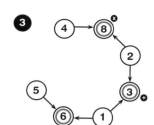 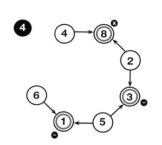

## Circuit Star

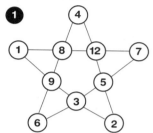 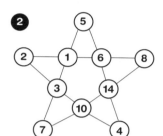 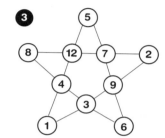 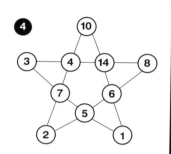

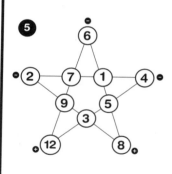 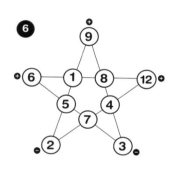 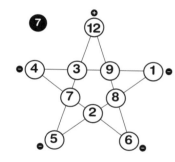 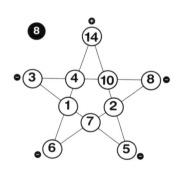

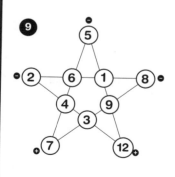 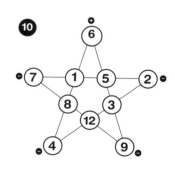 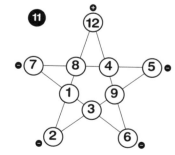 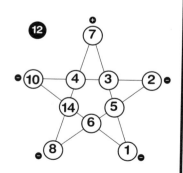